Praise for *The Naked Interview: Hiring Without Regret*

"I can speak from experience that HIRING is the toughest job as a business owner and ONE bad hire can cause YEARS of misery! Hiring has always been the biggest gamble and the biggest headache in all of my businesses. Finally somebody is tackling the core issues of this problem and giving some sane solutions. David your advice in hiring has helped immensely! Thanks for sharing your strategies!!!"

— Jim Worman, CEO/Entrepreneur

"Jensen nailed it. As a business and franchise owner myself, I found this book extremely valuable! As a business coach I loved David's pointers on decision and he's especially crystal clear on first evaluating what area you are hiring for. I know with this system my clients will benefit greatly and I will be referring back to this book often in the future."

— Todd Woods, Author of *Guerilla Marketing for Franchisees*

"David Jensen has developed a system that takes the guess work and finger-crossing out of the equation. In his Ten Truths, he summarizes the most important steps to take for hiring the right person to add to your team. His method of approach is easy to assimilate and he's got some great stories. *The Naked Interview* is a must read for executives that want to improve their business!"

— Eric Brackett, CEO of BTI Communications

D1407751

THE
NAKED
INTERVIEW

HIRING WITHOUT REGRET

By **David Jensen**

THE NAKED INTERVIEW
Hiring Without Regret

ISBN 978-1-61448-376-2 paperback
ISBN 978-1-61448-377-9 eBook
Library of Congress Control Number: 2012947959

Morgan James Publishing
The Entrepreneurial Publisher
5 Penn Plaza, 23rd Floor
New York City, New York 10001
(212) 655-5470 office • (516) 908-4496 fax
www.MorganJamesPublishing.com

In an effort to support local communities, raise awareness and funds, Morgan James Publishing donates a percentage of all book sales for the life of each book to Habitat for Humanity Peninsula and Greater Williamsburg.

Get involved today, visit
www.MorganJamesBuilds.com.

Other titles by David Jensen:

Get Hired! Interviewing Truths Revealed

Save Time & Money: Customer Service Secrets

THE NAKED INTERVIEW
HIRING WITHOUT REGRET

Table of Contents

Section III
Interviewing

Section IV
Selecting and Hiring

Section V – Bonus!
The Other Side of the Desk

"This book would not have made it to the printed page without the genuine help, efforts, and continued support of many."

Acknowledgements

This book would not have made it to the printed page without the genuine help, efforts, and continued support of many.

My wife, of twenty years and counting, and our children have endured countless years of my "brilliant" ideas, my late night scheming and writing, as well as my superfluous days of rambling on about helping others perfect their businesses and their lives, plus the importance of sharing expertise with business owners and executives at all levels.

My family has seen me travel the world following my passion. I spent nine weeks of business and government consulting in Buffalo, New York where it was nine below zero with about nine feet of snow the entire time. I was even bitten by a monkey at a business conference on the tropical island of Nevis, British West Indies. You *do not* want to have a tetanus shot there! All the while, my family never wavered in their love or tolerance.

Accolades are in order with endless love and respect for a few dynamic individuals who were my "partners-in-crime" along the way. My best friend and mentor, Gavin, is an indubitable hiring machine. Many of the experiences in this book occurred while he was sitting beside me laughing, thank goodness more *with* me than *at* me. Then Joyce and Lynda who have taught me invaluable lessons in caring for a business as if it were family, and for that I am forever grateful to them.

I couldn't overlook Kelli, the president of my company, a Rock of Gibraltar in completing this book itself and forging the launch of our business. It's all about caring, and she truly does. Keep an eye on us all at Naked Biz Solutions and The Hiring Academy; we are bettering the world, one executive and one business at a time.

Find out more about all of our business ventures and adventures at www.hiringacademy.com.

"I didn't want the regret of getting burned
in my friendships, relationships,
or business dealings."

Introduction

My Story

"Who called 9-1-1?" the policeman at the door asked.

I came out of the shadows at the top of the stairs, shaking, with tears streaming down my face. I was in cartoon pajamas, but wore my hockey helmet and held a baseball bat in my hand. A scared child was making a feeble attempt to defend himself.

"I did," I managed to blurt out between trembling sobs. The officer had a sudden realization looking at the situation and moved in front of my stepfather, asking him to exit the house immediately. My hero.

Growing up in an abusive household, I became socially introverted and distrustful of everyone around me. I never knew when I was going to say the wrong thing and get the backhand, the belt, or pushed into a wall and screamed at until I wet my pants. Even more painful, though, were the times I watched my mother take the brunt of my stepfather's brutality and I felt responsible. That's the reason I called the police that night, hoping that it wouldn't make it worse on her. She was overcome and invalidated to such a degree that I'm certain her only remaining will to live was looking out for her child. It wasn't until long after she bravely left him and eventually fell in love with someone who genuinely cared for her that I found enough peace to have a restful night's sleep.

I could never understand the reason she chose him in the first place. How could she not see his self-centered, controlling, dominating ways *before* she married him? Why didn't she consider his previous failed marriage as some indication of his character? Didn't she notice any indications of his contemptuous demeanor and scornful temper any sooner? Didn't she ask the right questions to find out if he was actually the right person with whom to spend the rest of her life? Was he that slick to cover his flaws during the dating process?

For some time, my life continued to be plagued with failures because of my continuing trend of bad-character judgment. This lack of foresight became apparent in my jilted romantic relationships and then in my poor choices of friends, mentors, and business partners. Life became a roller coaster of disappointments.

Reflecting later in life, I noticed the way the dating game mimics the interviewing process. One is being asked to meet someone and put his or her livelihood, or some portion of it, into that individual's hands. If you don't know the way to evaluate people or "interview" them, it's no wonder the divorce rate has soared beyond fifty percent.

Haven't we all heard from a friend or the media the disastrous way some company is headed as a result of it being poorly handled by *one* irresponsible employee?   Haven't we all decided never to eat at a certain restaurant again because the waiter was rude, or never shop at a specific store again because the clerk was inattentive? Worse yet, have you known a friend or associate so annoyed with a co-worker that he or she considered finding another job to avoid that one employee?   These scenarios could all be avoided if the hiring process was more thorough and predictable.

Approaching that ideal, though, took a guy like me turning a curse into a blessing.   It was really only a survival mechanism and the counseling of a genuine friend who led me down this path.   I couldn't afford to pick the wrong people in my life.   I didn't want the regret of getting burned in my friendships, relationships, or business dealings.   I found myself looking for a system that could screen for "trustworthiness" in relationships.   Learning so much about this attribute, I wanted to apply this workable truth to business.   While consulting hundreds of companies, I found this trait to be a *hot* topic.   Business owners, executives, and human resource (HR) personnel unanimously *hated* the hiring process. This discovery led to my developing a codified system of hiring that saved me and would save others from enduring the pain and regret of selecting the wrong people for their businesses.

I've achieved tremendous success since.   I have lived a few lives getting there, but what I've learned has been tried, tested and truly held up.   I am happily married for twenty years now, to my best friend and the love of my life.   I've been fortunate enough to have not only founded and owned a few of my own companies but along the way have consulted hundreds of others in organizing and expanding their businesses. I currently run a multi-million dollar producing company with clients earning billions. I enjoy sitting on the board of a few charitable organizations and for many years I've coached high school basketball at a championship level for "my exercise."

My purpose is to help business owners find and hire the right people so that they can pull back from their business and yet continue expanding!

Section I

WHY NAKED?

"Have you ever hired the first applicant
who interviewed for the job?"

One

Personnel Problems

**Dictionary.com defines Naked
(def. 12) in the following way:
plain-spoken; blunt:** *the naked truth.*

Embarking upon reading this book, you probably already have at least two questions or curiosities. One has to do with interviewing and hiring for your company and two, why The *Naked* Interview?

This book will answer your first question. As for the second, interviewing and hiring are not rocket science, but a sequential system of actions behind doing it successfully. I've codified this system.

As for the second question "why *naked?*" the answer is twofold. First is the obvious marketing pizzazz of using the word *naked* in the title. It does attract attention, right?

I also think the precise definition of *naked* will explain the reason why I chose this blatant adjective for the title of my book.

Being blunt expresses my strong feelings about revealing the bare (naked) truth of interviewing and hiring. It's important to me that one never commits the same errors I've made in business and in life by choosing the wrong person for the job or for some other role in life. I have observed the uncanny parallel nature of the hiring process to relationships of romance, friendship, and business.

I founded The Hiring Academy where we teach simple methods and provide workable tools for hiring the *right* people to help enhance businesses. This book will name the ten most important truths of hiring the best potential candidate. You'll view the raw data and some examples, but understand that this subject is a broad and continuous work-in-progress. Therefore, I'll make available a great deal of content on my website. This material has been developed to help you beyond the pages of this book. I'll continue to assist you as long as necessary. This expertise is my passion.

I am passionate about helping people with their hiring difficulties because I know how truly heart-wrenching and costly it can be to a business owner to discover later he or she made a disastrous decision in hiring. The flip side of this "coin" is seeing the thriving success of a business once it has implemented this codified system.

Have you ever hired the first applicant who interviewed for the job? Hired someone on whom you knew you were compromising? Hired the wrong person for whatever reason? Or worse, have you ever thought you hired the right person, only to discover later you were sorely mistaken?

Unfortunately, most business owners and HR professionals answer "yes" to these questions and live with the regrets of hiring mistakes with nothing more than a few horror stories and "lessons learned" to tell their friends. You might even have resigned yourself to thinking that it's just the luck of the draw or "you win some and you lose some." I'm here to tell you, that cliché is bogus. You never have to make these mistakes again in business or personal relationships. These answers can be found in this book as well.

The tools for evaluating applicants in this book are one hundred percent applicable to your interactions in everyday life. How do I know this? I used to experience the same challenges in my life but now I've mastered them. When I meet someone on the street, I rely on my observations and know about that person from the first impression. No doubt in my mind, you too, can learn this technique.

Personally, I could fill an encyclopedia with my own gross miscalculations of character and the failure to notice the obvious flaws in job candidates. These mistakes resulted in potentially millions of dollars in lost revenue and countless headaches.

Conversely, I've also seen a "diamond in the rough" get hired and this creating the most positive ripple effect in the work environment. That employee affirms not only the stabilizing of his or her own position but also the increasing productivity of others in the company. I've always joked with such employees, "I wish I could clone you." Have you ever said to an employee, "I wish I had ten of you?"

I began to wonder if potential employers could learn to isolate the exact characteristics, tendencies, traits, habits, and abilities that separated the competent and productive new hires from the PR paper-pushers and those who drain time, energy, and resources.

I badly needed this ability in order to survive in the competitive business world and I sought it out diligently; however, a simple solution didn't exist. There was no easy way to hire qualified people. Some companies pay a fortune and will use everything from a brain scan to a cavity search to examine the past of a potential candidate and match his or her past résumé of experience with a certain job description, but no one could predict the way a potential hiree will operate in the future as part of the team.

In my twenty-plus years of consulting with small business owners, corporate executives, and even politicians, I've clearly identified two uniformly troublesome areas for almost all businesses, namely, *marketing* and *personnel.* There are a lot of terrific marketing systems and advice out there but none could be well implemented without the right personnel.

This was never more obvious to me then the time one particular consulting client hired me to help organize an already successful telemarketing company. She was doing a couple million in profit but had plateaued. I quickly helped draft an organizing chart and standardized training materials for each job function, therefore increasing efficiency. However, the most valuable advice I gave her was with regards to her hiring of personnel. Up to that point she had been hiring the "usual suspects" whom were call-center employees who were nomadic between job to job opportunities and "knew it all" already. I encouraged her to cut-loose the attitude problems and take the slightly longer route of training more high dynamic, bright individuals. I'm certain this contributed to the fact that she later sold the company for around 40 million dollars.

Here are some of the questions to which most employers unfortunately answer *yes*. Ask yourself the following questions:

> Have you had little success in finding and hiring capable employees?

> Do newly hired employees seem not to train quickly and function well at their jobs?

> Do you find yourself solving problems that should be handled by employees?

> How productive are your employees, really?

> Is the morale in your company just not that high?

The uncertainty of finding and choosing the right people plagues everyone from business relationships to personal commitments. What separates the heartbreaks and heartaches from the loving and caring of a successful couple? What factors lead down that disastrous road to "Why did I invest so much time and effort into loving him?" or that regretful feeling of "She's the one that got away."

Pieces of reliable information are available. Decent texts are written on some of the elements discussed here. However, no standard approach is documented in any one location with all of the necessary tools and advice. Therefore, I planned to accomplish that feat. I am passionate about the information I found. I know many people and business owners are experiencing the same challenges I did in finding qualified people to hire or simply the right people to be in their lives. I'll provide sound advice to ease the pain of hiring and lessen the chance of sleepless nights, seemingly irreversible damage, and those regretful words, "If I only knew then, what I know now."

The Naked Interview: Hiring Without Regret is the book in which I tell my story, share my mistakes, acknowledge my successes, as well as provide my findings and my system to help business owners find, interview, and hire the *right* employees. My advice was earned from hard-won experience. I've developed a process with methods, examples, checklists, tests, and questionnaires, all to aid an employer in eliminating the bad, avoiding the ugly, and hiring good employees to succeed.

Thanks for reading this book. I know the information can benefit you. Once you've completed it there are constantly updated tips & tools and a plethora of shared knowledge at my website www.hiringacademy.com.

"These ten truths are valid, proven, essential,
and worthy of being clearly stated."

Two

Ten Naked Truths
for Employers

These truths have been the prominent
guides to my success.

The information in this chapter is *vital* (defined as necessary to life). My decades of interviewing and hiring experience have culminated in the development of my hiring system, this book, and these ten truths, the bare (naked) truths.

Please take note; I did not title this chapter "The" Ten Truths, but simply Ten Truths. You may have adopted other truths from experience or assimilated them from other sources. However, these truths have been the prominent guides to my success in hiring the crème de la crème. These truths are valid, proven, essential, and worthy of being clearly stated.

Truth One

Use Diligence, Not Desperation

Never rush into hiring a prospective candidate. Use diligence, not desperation. This truth means that while you probably needed to hire someone yesterday or months ago, you still need to hire *carefully.*

Many expenses and legal obligations are assumed upon hiring a new member of the team; therefore, don't roll the dice indiscriminately.

Business and personal factors are also involved. Upon being hired, this new employee is going to be visible every day. He or she is going to bring a specific personality to the workplace, for better or worse. This temperament will affect you and the existing staff; the "newbie" will now be part of your lives.

It bodes well not to act in desperation. Grant more importance to doing your homework and finding a better fit. Don't merely hire any "warm body." A little diligence will save a significant amount of time in the long run.

Truth Two

Phone Screening: You Should "Hear" Them Smile

When phone screening, you should "hear" that prospective hiree smile. Funny but true, and, yes, you *can* tell. You only have to be an attentive listener.

A definite giveaway would be, while talking to that individual, *you* are smiling, too. If the candidate is upbeat and genuinely interested, his or her smile will be contagious.

In this brief phone screening all you are looking for is do they sound professional and create a desire for you to officially interview him or her. A phone screening should be kept short. This conversation is not an interview; it is merely a call to see if the applicant will be invited to interview as the next step in the hiring process.

Pay attention to the background noise, the candidate's manners, and the way he or she communicates. For example, does that person interrupt and not let you get a word in edgewise? It should be a smooth, polite conversation that ends in setting an appointment or not.

Truth Three

Testing Tells the True Tale

Oh, the regret of being fooled. Testing tells the true tale.

Believe it or not, some people talk a good game, but don't have the experience or products to support it. Tests rarely lie.

An employer will want to know the intelligence level of the candidate and also use the test for general personality. Aptitude tests exist for general workplace competence and industry-specific knowledge. This testing will easily separate the highly trained from the inexperienced.

I've developed a proven testing system that can help an employer narrow down the candidates logically. If you don't use this system, use another, but definitely use some type of testing.

Truth Four

An Interview is a Tug-of-War; so Pull

An interview is a tug-of-war; so "pull" the information you want to know.   It won't always be offered voluntarily.   Seek answers to your questions and follow up on any statement that you don't understand or doesn't make sense.

I'm not saying everyone you interview has skeletons in his or her closet, but if that candidate is looking for a new job, usually there is some story you should know.   At the very least, give that potential hiree the opportunity to lay his or her cards on the table. That way the prospective candidate won't walk around embarrassed or insecure, always wondering whether or not you know their well-kept secrets.   Otherwise, that person might make the same mistakes elsewhere and thus begins the potential candidate's demise.

Pull the data to discover anything you need to know, up front, so that a prospective hiree can start with a clean slate.   For all you know, at the last job he or she burned down the break room.

Truth Five

Creative Questions Get the Answers You Really Want

Candidates usually come prepared for the usual interview questions and they won't reveal any genuine display of emotion when you ask, "What did you like about your last job?"

You will, however, gain some insight when you ask the following questions: "To what sport would you equate your last job? What position did you play in it? Where do you see the industry going in the next five-to-ten years? How do you see yourself contributing to our success?"

The candidate's true interest, intelligence, and personality level can't help but be revealed. Creative questions get the answers you really want.

Truth Six

The Tour Isn't Show and Tell; It's Watch and Listen

Another test of a candidate's team compatibility is the company tour.

The tour isn't show and tell; on the contrary, it's watch and listen. A great deal can be learned along the way by listening to a prospective candidate's comments and observing his or her interactions with the staff.

> Is the candidate respectful and polite?

> Does he or she seem "overly" friendly?

> Does the candidate ask meaningful questions?

> Does the prospective hiree look overwhelmed by the whole environment?

Observe closely. Evaluate the way he or she fits in with your office "family."

Truth Seven

Trust Your "Gut Feeling"

Sometimes, you've got to go with your intuition.

The importance of the way someone makes you "feel" is paramount to his or her ability to strike a balance. It also determines how much the company is willing to invest in a new employee. This investment establishes the candidate's "worth" in your eyes.

If your gut says this prospective hiree could work out great, go the extra mile to make it happen. If your gut is uncertain and queasy, you're more likely to be looking for reasons that candidate will fail. Make sense? Trust your "gut feeling", always.

Truth Eight

Personality Is Found the Second Time Around

Always bring prospects back for multiple interviews. The second date is easy to land after charming someone, but the third one always seems to be a more difficult commitment.

So goes the second interview. I am always surprised, sometimes shocked, by the applicant who shows up for the additional interview. It's often barely the same person with whom you spoke previously. Personality is found the second time around.

Some candidates figure they can "let their guard down." They dress down and relax their personalities since they've already been interviewed. This relaxation often reveals their true colors and makes any decision quite easy.

Conversely, the second interview could put you totally at ease. Their nervous jitters have disappeared, their strengths are confidently shining through, and you receive the reassurance for which you are looking.

Truth Nine

You *Gotta* Grill the References

Think of the distance you'd go for a friend, and so would the "buddy" of the applicant providing a reference.

Be absolutely certain you talk to the right person, not only friends listed on the résumé. Supervisors from previous positions are the most valuable sources of accurate performance-related information. You then *gotta* grill the references.

Be sure to ask pointed questions to determine the supervisor's genuine feelings about the candidate. Be aware it may be the words he or she *doesn't* say that are most important. Be attentive that the feeling you're seeking may not always be communicated with words; sometimes it's merely the tone of voice. HR departments often are litigation-shy and pare down the facts if an employee's departure was less than ideal. However, the guard comes down with well-prepared questions.

Obviously a sterling candidate will be openly praised and you might even hear the magic words, "They will always have a job here."

Truth Ten

Selecting and Hiring Should Be Easy

In reality, the person accepting the job is much more nervous about "the hire" than you are. You are in control; therefore, selecting and hiring should be easy and straightforward.

Multiple interviews, tests, and your comfort level will narrow down the candidates so you're able to select the right person for the job.

Decide on the best-suited candidate by using the tools at your disposal. If during the initial training period you come to find you chose incorrectly, let the individual go his or her merry way and you move on.

In summary: If you use these proven truths as guidelines for the hiring process you'll achieve greater success with your company's expansion. Use these steps to choose the best prospective candidate, while saving time, energy, and money.

These truths are available as a free download at www.hiringacademy.com.

Section II

DECIDING TO HIRE

"Consider first the exhaustive expenses of replacing an employee with a new hire."

Three

Evaluate Your Needs

**Define the business's needs carefully
and the way that translates to the addition
of a new employee, and then proceed.**

What comes before interviewing candidates?

Determine by careful inspection and evaluation the actual need to hire. Drawing from decades of experience consulting with business owners, let me assure you, it can be a bigger mistake to hire someone who is not needed in the first place than hiring an ineffective candidate.

Consider first the exhaustive expenses of replacing someone with a new employee. In the United States, the National Labor Board estimates it costs between 1.5 to 3.5 times an employee's annual salary to replace that person. That Board averages the cost of the new hiring process alone at around $15,000 each time a company hires a new employee. It is easy to overlook the impact of that cost. Examine the following items for greater insight:

Advertising costs

HR staffing costs

Interviewing time

Reference-checking time

Salary, of course

Any relocation costs

Training costs

Employee problems with low morale

Incomplete assignments

Potential customer problems

Lost profit margins

These areas vary from business to business, but the common thread remains the same. It's *expensive* to hire, train, and replace personnel. That cost is only one of the many reasons to do it correctly the first time.

To Hire or Reorganize

The reasons for needing more personnel could probably fill an ocean. For now let me divulge a couple secrets to ensure you're hiring someone for the right reasons before embarking on this hiring venture.

Understandably this task isn't so difficult if you have a retail business with rotating shifts of hourly employees. However, where the need isn't so specific, it's important to have good, reliable justification for expanding the team.

Before interviewing, focus on the importance of saving time and money. Define the business's needs carefully and the way that translates to the addition of a new employee, and then proceed. You owe it to the company to be certain of this need first.

Often times extra personnel are hired for the wrong reason, sometimes to pick-up the dropped balls or the ignored functions that aren't sufficiently being handled by others. One employee could be covering up a camouflaged hole created by another. At this point the employee claims to be fully handling one or more responsibilities, when in reality the job duties are falling through the cracks. You had thought one employee could do the job but now you need to hire additional help. Maybe one person could do the job, but not the one currently employed.

I'd suggest starting out by naming or listing the functions that will be covered by a new hiree. Then with that list consider the following points before initiating the hiring process:

Has the position been vacant long?

Has the vacancy created any problems, or could the company actually thrive without someone in this position?

Are there jobs or functions that could actually be covered by an existing employee?

Are there duties supposed to be covered by another but you don't trust that employee to do them?

What was the reason for the change? Was it a promotion, transfer, or termination?

Let's look at it this way. Often eight responsibilities can be handled by a position and the existing employee is only handling four of them, although that person may actually be capable of handling them all. Often an employer makes the common mistake of hiring a new person to handle the other four functions. What a waste of valuable resources.

It's a vicious cycle that only management can handle by stepping back and truly evaluating the need. Jack is only able to handle four of his eight responsibilities, but if I put Jill there, all eight would be completed with time to spare. If that's a fact, then cut Jack loose and increase Jill's responsibilities plus her pay by ten to twenty percent. You saved not only the payroll of one employee but also rewarded a deserving worker for doing her job. It's all about economics and efficiency. You may also increase the whole area's production by raising morale. Coworkers already knew about Jack's lack of accomplishment long before you became aware.

I see examples of inefficient staff utilization in many of the businesses with which I consult and hear about this problem all the time. For example, I was recently in Costa Rica talking to a friend who mentioned he was selling his company. Knowing the industry, I asked him the most revealing questions right away. How much gross income do you make and then more important, how many employees do you have? Interestingly, the amount of income was the same as another company with which I'd had experience.

When he answered the second question, I was surprised to hear the number of employees was *double* that of the other company. This number means that twice as much of his profits were being consumed by salaries and overhead. I knew this fact was true because the other company was producing the same income with half the employees, resulting in much greater profits.

This problem is all too often the case and screams that inefficiencies are rampant within a company. If he had evaluated this aspect of his business and handled the distribution of workload, he probably wouldn't be selling his company because he'd be enjoying a stellar increase in profitability. I shared these observations with him and tailored a consulting program to accelerate his profits that will increase the value of the company for its sale or maybe entice him to keep his newly improved enterprise.

Evaluating actual need is probably the most overlooked aspect of the hiring process. Use the appropriate time and attention to ensure you find, in detail, what's really needed, or not, before you dive into interviews.

"After evaluating the company's needs you can now define an exact job description."

Four

Decide, Promote, Recruit

Don't "settle" on a candidate.
Develop a large pool of candidates
from whom to choose.

Along the way, in doing business and living life, I've learned one invaluable lesson that outshines them all. This action alone I found to be of the utmost importance and ever infallible. The power of *decision*.

You may roll your eyes and say, "I've heard it all before" and think "sure, I already do that." And you do, but have you ever examined the power of that decision? It's even easier to see in the reverse. I can think of many times when I "tried" to accomplish a goal but didn't have a clear decision about it before I began. You can guess what happened, nothing.

Here's a simple exercise, to my point. Think of something significant you've accomplished. Now remember the first time you started working on that goal. Good. Think back to the moment you actually *decided* you were going to achieve that one objective. You became excited again, didn't you? That moment of *decision*, that clear picture of yourself accomplishing that goal, *is* the main reason you were able to complete it in the first place.

My wife and I make lists all the time. "We need to get this or that done, we want this, wouldn't it be nice to have that," and so on. Then, inevitably those lists are lost in a drawer or filed in a documents folder on a laptop never to be seen again. Have you ever done that sort of thing? What's really cool is eventually finding those lists. It could be a month later, six months after the fact, sometimes longer and sure enough what do you find? Most of the items on the list have been *completed*. It all lies in the decision.

Recently, I was having lunch with a friend and she shared with me her serendipitous example of "making a list". As a teenager she had playfully, but honestly, written down all the qualities she wanted in a man to spend the rest of her life with. Then one day, years later, she was walking hand-in-hand with her husband and was pleasantly surprised to remember that list. She realized that he, in fact, had all of those desired qualities.

Maybe you compiled a list when deciding the type of person you'd like to date and later looked back and saw the one holding your hand and thought, wow, this is the person I always dreamed I'd be with. Realize that sometimes we may decide to be with the wrong people, too.

Here's another scenario, albeit a less significant one, my beloved sports car. I can remember the times I began daydreaming about the type of car I wanted "when I could afford it." This wasn't just one dream or decision but a series of narrowing down the exact qualities of the perfect car for me. It went from sports car, to luxury sports car, to black luxury sports car, to fast black luxury sports car, to a fast black Jaguar luxury sports car. Alas, one day there it was parked in my driveway: a 400-horsepower, supercharged luxury beast, a Jaguar XJR. I reflected with admiration, having finally bought the exact car I'd decided I wanted so long ago.

How does this lesson on decision relate to hiring? Every business owner, every HR executive, everyone needing to hire anyone (yes you) needs to decide first that you *are* going to find the right person to join your team. Start with a clear image of the perfect candidate.

> What skills should that person possess?

> What experience does he or she have?

> What does that prospective employee look and act like?

Watch out, when you define that candidate exactly, he or she might actually walk right in the door. Decide today and make tomorrow that much better.

Define the job description thoroughly; it's well worth the time and attention to detail. Part of evaluating the company's needs is really looking at the amount this new hire will actually contribute to the bottom line. The new employee's salary should be commensurate with that amount.

After evaluating the company's needs you can now define an exact job description. You will draft a "Now Hiring" advertisement with certainty because you have fully mapped out the company's needs and the desired candidate. This will uncork a rapid flow of applications

The Internet is the foremost resource to place job ads in this age of technology. Dozens of sites will promote the job listing to thousands of people with the talents you require. These sites include LinkedIn, Monster Jobs.com, Yahoo Jobs, and CareerBuilder, to mention a few.

It makes sense that the more candidate résumés you receive, the better your chances of hiring the right employee for the job. You'll create a big pool of options from which to choose, so there's a greater likelihood you'll find a better fit. Quantity and quality result from promoting broadly. Go to great lengths to find the perfect candidate.

One night, my colleague and good friend, Gavin, and I heard about a local business mixer. We were really under the gun to meet a deadline of finding a new hotshot sales representative. We arrived at the door excited about joining the party and finding a potential recruit, only to be abruptly stopped by a "brick house" of a doorman. "Mr. Gigantic" quickly informed us, "No costume, no entry." We didn't even make it in the door! So it was time for Plan B. We had to find a way into that party or we'd miss the opportunity to meet the menagerie of new talent.

We were definitely not surrendering to defeat. A light bulb went off as we spotted a neighboring convenience store. Plan B was improvisation. A quick trip across the street, and ten minutes later we walked out with a plastic badge, handcuffs, and cap gun; one of us loses the suit coat and tie for a leather jacket from the trunk and we returned as Tango and Cash. Whatever it takes, right?

Two hours and a dozen prospects later, we excused ourselves to the back patio with a top candidate and sealed the deal right then and there. She started her new employment and career the next day.

If you're aggressive, you'll find a multitude of suitable applicants. I will applaud your innovation and it will bring your wish to fulfillment.

The bottom line is promoting is extremely important. You never know who is looking for a job. You need to promote and advertise the available position so potential employees can find you and vice versa. Don't "settle" on a prospective candidate if you know the qualifications you want and have a large pool from whom to choose. Most important, don't be afraid to hold out for the perfect choice.

"You have promoted the job opening a great deal and should be barraged by an influx of résumés."

Five

Pare Down the Prospects

Products are actual, completed actions or activities taken to a finished result or a "done deal."

You have promoted the job opening a great deal and should be barraged by an influx of résumés. Sort through those résumés by simply making organized piles. Good-looking prospects on the left, absolute pass on the right and those with something of interest, but you're not sure about, in the middle. Then decide the applicants with whom you want to have a first conversation with via phone- screening. You'll have be looking for obvious important factors such as the following:

Does that potential candidate have experience?

Has he or she held the same or similar position elsewhere?

Check out the applicant's track record of employment history. Has that potential hiree spent the last ten years hopping from job to job?

Has he or she worked continuously in this same field or is this a career change?

Does he or she show stability with previous employers?

If that applicant did stay at a job for a longer period, was there any advancement or increase in responsibilities?

Phone-screening

Start calling the candidates. Don't think for a minute that you should invite every applicant in for an interview just because his or her résumé is attractive. The initial phone conversation with these candidates can provide a significant amount of eye-opening information.

Screening candidates by phone helps narrow the field. This process can be tedious as there are many outgoing and incoming telephone calls. The conversations themselves can also be deceptive but will save a great deal of time in the long run as you'll eliminate some potential time-wasting interviews.

Once the candidate's on the telephone ask a couple crucial questions. This conversation is not the time to conduct an entire interview. You'll be surprised how much information can be gathered with a short phone conversation. The following are some non-optimum points to watch for:

> The person hesitates or pauses before every answer.

> The candidate sounds preoccupied with some other activity while talking to you.

> The person does not really answer the question, but veers off in another direction.

> The candidate has to consult his or her résumé in order to answer your questions.

> That prospective employee acts as if he or she has another job secured and you're less important.

Good signs present themselves as well and include the following:

> The candidate seems genuinely pleased to hear from you.

> The potential employee has been expecting your call and is prepared to talk.

He or she knows about you and your company.

This prospective hiree reveals a high interest in the company and the position.

Thank the candidate at the end of each phone call and let him or her know that this call is an initial phone-screening and you'll be calling back, if selected, to arrange an interview time. This call provides the opportunity to look at your notes from the initial phone screening, and compare them to the candidate's résumé.

All of this information may seem tedious and perhaps a bit unnecessary if you've never been this thorough in the past. However, since you're reading this book, then you may have been experiencing personnel problems or be looking to end distressing turnover that has been haunting your business for years.

When referring to your notes, look for the same items as the first time you read that person's résumé. However, this time see if it corresponds with the phone-screening information.

I want to share a story of a business owner I helped to escape the downward spiral of hiring bad employees that led to massive profit loss for him and his franchise. While consulting, I have encountered many businesses with similar problems stemming from simply having the wrong personnel or having the right personnel in the wrong positions.

I was in Buffalo, New York in December. It's such a beautiful city during spring and summer but a frozen tundra during winter. I endured nine weeks of nine-below-zero temperatures and nine feet of snow. I was wrapping up a project in the area doing introductory consulting interviews with small business owners. I eagerly agreed to these interviews to help stimulate the local economy, since the owner of our consulting firm hailed from a Buffalo suburb. Despite the elements, I consulted more than a hundred business owners and executives in the area, including the mayor himself.

On one particular day my firm had me in the owner's "office" (a converted stockroom off the kitchen) of a popular coffee and donut shop. I was scheduled to do a brief introductory interview, or so I thought, to give the owner a couple pointers, and perhaps sell him a consulting package.

This fellow was a genuine Canadian, friendliest man in the world, complete with a Canadian accent and interspersed "ehs." He was also around 6'5" a *big guy*. He greeted me with a warm handshake and a bear hug. I really liked this guy and wanted to help him. While discussing areas in which he could become more efficient, he mentioned bringing someone from another location to handle an open position. I asked, "How many locations do you have?" Whereupon he told me that he's the biggest franchise-holder, with twelve stores in New York State. In addition, he also owns thirty Canadian stores. That's a tremendous amount coffee and donuts for a "small" business.

That number of stores requires hundreds of employees and, therefore, he was encountering numerous problems with personnel; making effective hiring a *big* concern for this *big guy* to run his *big* business efficiently.

In many years of consulting, I've isolated only two primary areas that if not properly handled can actually cause a business to fail.

Conversely, if handled well, these two areas all but guarantee success, namely, *marketing* and *personnel.*

This guy obviously had marketing down to a science as the place was packed.   Not coincidentally, most franchises do, as they usually have cookie-cutter marketing programs to accelerate their expansion.   It was, therefore, no surprise the shade of green he turned as we spoke of employee difficulties.   We estimated his losing thousands of dollars every month exclusively the result of personnel problems.

Recognizing the problem and the importance of solving it, I started him on the entire line-up of executive training with a strong emphasis on personnel processing, testing, and hiring.   I walked out into the snow with a new client whose business would now be saved.   Weird that while trudging through the snow back to my car, it seemed remarkably warm that day.

Behind the scenes, we came to find his HR department was not really screening the applicants coming into the office.   Had the HR personnel asked the right questions, they never would have hired half of the people who later failed.   My big Canadian friend learned his lesson and made sure his hiring department understood this process well.

Upon completion of his program and to this day, his business has maintained a stable increase of profitability and his personnel headaches have lessened tremendously.   This success allowed him to surpass his goals and become the number-one franchise-holder in the world for that particular brand.

Look for Products

Products are completed actions or activities taken to a final result or a "done deal." In other words, people need to prove having actually accomplished those things they've taken credit for.

I had an interesting experience once when asked to do some consulting for a classic automobile restoration shop. This once-thriving business was really in danger of closing its doors and needed to solve a grave problem.

I asked my client when the shop first started noticing a decline in business. It appeared the trouble began when it hired the most recent employee. He had claimed on his résumé a major car restoration accomplishment. Upon further investigation it turns out that two other applicants claimed to have restored the same car. We had to trace back to the source in order to find the truth.

I called each of these men and started asking some detailed questions about that particular restoration job on which each had staked his claim. One had only applied the decals, one had only worked at the shop hired to do the project, and the other was the genuine professional who had restored that vehicle to perfection.

Who had the shop actually hired? Mr. decal guy had been the lucky candidate. He certainly was a fine employee with his particular skill but he didn't have the depth of knowledge to manage an entire project from start to finish and for that reason the business started failing.

Due diligence will take an employer a great distance. First, ask yourself the right questions so you know the ideal candidate you want to interview. Use phone-screening for a couple important questions *before* he or she interviews, and last, ask about actual products from his or her previous jobs. This careful approach will help pare down the prospects and provide a relevant selection of candidates from which to choose.

Section III

INTERVIEWING

"Manners and professionalism are paramount as the company representative placed in the role of hiring."

Six

The Interview

Determine if the candidate possesses
the necessary knowledge for the job.

Hiring is easily likened to getting married and interviewing is much like dating. It can be difficult to find "the one." You don't want to jump right into bed with the first person you meet or at least don't want to marry that individual after the first date.

The point here is that appearances up front may not always be genuine. It would best suit you to become familiar with the individual first and figuratively meet the parents, too. People may bring baggage to a relationship, for better or worse. You might have to compromise on some points or let it be known up front that you won't concede.

This impression begins from the moment a candidate arrives. In fact, I have a friend who heads an attorneys' office specializing in employment law and litigation for employers. The candidates are watched on camera from the moment they walk from the parking lot, step into the elevator, and enter the reception area. My friend said people would be shocked by the mannerisms seen when someone doesn't know he or she is being watched. Not that picking one's nose is going to cause that candidate to lose the job but the point here is to use every moment possible to be looking for genuine character.

Specific steps are used in conducting the interview, which will follow. First, however, I want to mention "Courtesy interviews" that help avoid wasting either party's valuable time.

Courtesy interviews and a code word add a little fun to the process and save time. In a business in which I was vice president over the human resource division, we used the code word "coffee" to provide an indication of the current candidate's standing in an interview.

It went something like this: if a candidate arrived to interview who was obviously not a good fit for the company as a result of unprofessional appearance, attire, conduct, or presentation, the receptionist called HR and told them the interviewee had arrived, and by the way, don't try the coffee in the kitchen; it's cold and bitter today.

This clue alerted HR that the person currently standing in reception was now placed in the category of a "courtesy interview." HR's procedure then sped up significantly. Instead of handing the person an application that requires twenty minutes to complete or giving him

or her a wasted tour that exposes this candidate to the entire company, the applicant is taken straight to the interview room. There, he or she is greeted and told that the company is seeing so many candidates that the interviewer has to breeze through the preliminary consultations, so please excuse the rush.

Here one would, cut to the chase with a couple significant questions, such as the reason that applicant thinks he or she is right for the job and the qualifications that candidate brings to the table, asking if he or she has done this same job previously (which is often the easy out). "Sorry, we're looking for more of X, Y or Z, but we'll keep your résumé on file." If you are uncomfortable saying no in this manner, you can always say the position has already been filled or you're seeing several candidates in the next couple days, and if he or she doesn't hear from you, we went in another direction. Thank you; let me show you the way out. This truncated method works effectively and saves everyone time.

The Interview Sequence

Welcome the candidate. Introduce yourself. Let the applicant know your position in the company, and that today is only the first interview. Ensure the consultation is held in a private location with a professional atmosphere. Conduct it in a conference room or office where you will be undisturbed. Keep the first interview short, preferably not longer than fifteen or twenty minutes.

In the first impression, note whether or not the candidate looks you in the eye when talking. This one never fails. If it is so uncomfortable for a candidate to look me in the eye during a conversation, especially in an interview, then I know I won't be comfortable having that potential candidate in my organization. They may not be able to look a customer in the eye and gain their trust. It is one of those observations that has always proven true over the years.

Begin with easy social questions, such as:

Was it easy to find our office?

Would you like some water or coffee?

Then explain the way the company operates and the responsibilities of the job. Remember to take notes during the interview or directly after the candidate leaves the room. Taking notes during the interview will demonstrate genuine interest in that applicant as a prospect.

Invite the candidate to ask questions about the company and about the work he or she might be expected to do if hired. Be clear and direct in your communication. Observe whether or not the candidate's interest increases during the interview.

Pay attention to whether or not the candidate appears motivated or enthusiastic. You want only candidates who are willing and eager to make a positive difference in the company.

Use questions that create the necessity for the candidate to think independently and answer honestly, rather than use some rote script from a book or the redundant coaching received from a personnel agency. Be creative and force that person to think out of the box.

Realize you are not looking for all of the interviewees to be cookie-cutter, rote or robotic renditions of each other. Individuality is an important characteristic for this potential applicant and should be in your search as well. You want to be able to see them for who they really are see through any phoniness.

Ask some of the following questions:

> Why do you want this job?

> Now that you understand a few details about this job and the responsibilities it may entail, are you more or less interested and why?

> Have you previously worked or always wanted to work in this particular field?

What experience qualifies you to be the best possible candidate for this position?

What is the number-one factor that sways you one way or the other in looking for a job? Salary? Job duties? Your boss?

What ambitions do you have regarding your level of achievement in this prospective new job?

What are your career goals?

What personality traits would you prefer your boss have or not have?

Be alert to "red flags" in the candidate's attitude. Is it superficial or is he or she really motivated to be hired? Does salary seem to be the candidate's main concern or only motivation, or does this applicant actually reveal interest in the position? At the end of the day, does this prospective candidate seem genuinely satisfied with the conditions of the job?

These questions are relevant to selecting the most appropriate candidate.

Is the Candidate Qualified

Check the prospective candidate's education, training, and experience closely. Review the prospect's professional background, and for each job he or she has had, ask the applicant the reason he or she ended employment there? Let the candidate explain any possible "holes" in his or her career timeline as well.

Stay in control of the interview and pay extra attention not to let the candidate diverge from the subject. Discuss the candidate's previous career.

> Did he or she hold a job regularly or only sporadically?

> Did the applicant leave the earlier employment before a replacement was found, or without making it easy for the replacement to take control of the new duties?

Be aware if the candidate is critical of his or her previous employer. This criticism is a big red flag. If this person is so unhappy with a previous employer and willing to bash that person on the spot, there is definitely unfinished business and baggage that will carry over into the new employment, not to mention this applicant's unprofessional criticism.

Practical Knowledge

Determine if the candidate has the necessary knowledge for the job. Ask technical questions, too. You can verify their familiarity with the terminology and job-specific procedures by asking for examples of their previous products.

Listen for practical examples revealing the candidate's competence. Be alert for dissertations that sound like things he or she "knows you want to hear." This charade also becomes apparent when the candidate doesn't display certainty in answering questions and providing solutions. It is also revealing if he or she gives answers that seem unnecessarily complicated as if this candidate can't get his or her own story straight.

Has This Candidate Produced Results?

It is vital to check the candidate's ability to achieve results. Is the prospect able to translate his or her knowledge into definite results of value? You need to know about that person's earlier products. Then to effectively verify this, check references after the interview.

The following are some recommended questions to ask candidates:

> What achievements in earlier jobs make you proud?

Tell me about projects for which you were responsible and their outcomes.

Tell me about results expected of you and the way they turned out.

How could your results be measured?

What did you do to achieve these results?

What do you think is the most important attribute necessary to achieving results?

Did you work at a steady pace?

How was your productivity and efficiency compared with others?

Whom did you report to?

Can that person confirm the information you have given here?

Have you had a job in which you did not achieve good enough results? If yes, why? (The answer he or she gives on this question could be revealing. Did he or she own up to a fault? Most important, did that candidate learn a lesson from it?)

What is your former employer likely to say about you?

You can use the last one in reference checking. When you call a former supervisor, mention the candidate's answer and gauge the former employer's response.

Every applicant is going to give his or her best "spin" on performance at previous jobs. The following are the questions to ask yourself about each prospective candidate's answers.

How enthusiastic does the candidate appear to be when talking about previous results?

Does he or she know the way the results were achieved?

Is the person capable of pinpointing definite previous results?

Does he or she describe the previous results in a theoretical or a practical manner?

Can those results be verified?

The Interview Is a Tug of War

During the interview, the majority of fact-finding will occur, as this will be the basis for your decision, interview thoroughly. Bona fide tenacity here will save major headaches later.

Start with the candidate's résumé and pick it apart without remorse. Go through each employer, educational achievement, and other sections with a fine-toothed comb. Retrieve names and specific details.

> What was your supervisor?
> To what extent were you 'responsible' for all of the duties?
>
> What was your salary that year?
>
> Did you expand this area and become an asset?
>
> What was the specific reasoning behind your lay-off or leaving?
>
> With whom can I verify this information?

Once your questions are answered, don't commit to hiring, not in the same moment at least.

Manners and professionalism are paramount as the company's representative placed in the role of hiring. Good people are drawn toward others who appear professional and stable. When a prospective candidate is interviewing for the job, he or she is also hoping to see if his or her future would be secure in taking a job with the company. You, too, must put your best foot forward. I guarantee this will help you procure the best new employee.

Once, and only once, I made the embarrassing mistake of "being funny" while conducting a hiring interview by telling a woman we administer personality tests to match the co-workers and make certain we weren't adding someone to the team who was going to "go postal". She looked at me and with a deadpan smile and stated that her husband was a United States postal worker. She wasn't kidding and didn't think I was funny. I was flabbergasted and embarrassed, to say the least. The point is, *be professional.* I should simply have stated that a personality test illustrates the way people really view themselves.

I'm sure you won't make the same error in judgment. However, will one of your HR staff?

Have your HR staff trained and drilled, yes drilled, on the way to do a proper and thorough job interview with a prospective candidate. Include in this training, the way to represent the company as professionally as possible and present any scenarios that may occur. If any of these suggestions seem a bit much, I assure you they're not. All of this thoroughness on your part as a business owner or HR department interviewer will genuinely allow you to find that perfect addition to the company.

Look for the way a prospective candidate answers tough questions that arise, questions about management in particular, and any bad reports he or she might have heard. Make sure everyone is on the same page. Know when should you extend an interview to dig deeper and when should you break out the "courtesy interview". This thinking on your feet will ensure interviews are the correct length of time dependent on the candidate's qualifications.

There should be an exact pattern or routine in which all interviews are conducted. If Michael in HR interviews a prospective candidate, his results will be the same at the conclusion which Sherry the vice president would have achieved if interviewing the same candidate. When you have a system that is effective, then you've made the interviewing process a science.

Trust That "Gut Feeling"

Your "gut feeling" or intuition can be a useful tool in quickly evaluating the individual with the least disparity from other methods. However, some guidelines should be pursued when following your intuition.
First of all, does your gut tell you this candidate is a great person who's going to be a long-term asset to the company and do you feel positive vibes from him or her? Or does your stomach a bit get queasy? Are you wondering whether or not you're having the wool pulled over your eyes or the sense that you're acting too hastily?

I'm a believer in the fact that *you just know.*

Immediately upon meeting someone, you're at ease or you're not. You trust or you don't. You feel a friendship and camaraderie or you don't. I'm sure you can recall examples of this both ways. Everyone has a friend who double-crossed him or her in the long run and that unfortunate regretful feeling later of "I knew it." The opposite can also be true; the boss or pal was genuine. From the moment you met him or her, a symbiosis existed and it has never been proven wrong.

Before trusting your gut, make sure it's awake. Be certain you're not tired, hungry, upset, or rushed. These factors could affect the clarity of your gut instinct.

Does the candidate sound too good to be true? Oftentimes that is the case. One of the greatest complaints from employers is that "So-and-so interviewed so wonderfully and then flaked" or "We had so much faith in him or her that it was a shock to see his or her real self."

The Tour Isn't Show and Tell; It's Watch and Listen

A tour of the facility can be one of the most important steps in selecting a candidate and the most time saving part of the process.

Introduce yourself to the applicant upon arrival and provide a little reassurance, such as "I remember speaking to you on the phone; you sounded sharp." Or "I was impressed with your résumé, I'm glad to meet you in person." This remark validates him or her and establishes a personal rapport to relax any defenses that prospect might have. It also provides a better picture of your own personality and not just a front for interviewing.

You can start the interview with a company tour of the facility or wait until after talking with the candidate to see if he or she interviews well. The tour establishes a sense of reality for the candidate of the actual workplace and provides a picture of the genuine work environment, for better or worse.

A real professional can tell from the tour alone whether or not an applicant is a likely candidate for hire. On the tour you should observe the obvious clues such body language and demeanor.

> Does the potential employee wrinkle his or her nose at the prospect of having a cubicle for an office?

> Does he or she greet others along the way with friendly manners and respect?

> Does the candidate ask educated questions?

> Or does he or she act as if they "know-it-all"?

These observations can determine a potential prospect or not, from the beginning.

At the conclusion of the tour ask the candidate, "Does this seem like the type of work environment in which you'd be comfortable?" Or "Can you picture yourself working here?" Or simply ask the candidate, "What's your first impression?"

If you have a plan for the interview, focus on asking the right questions, and know the answers that you're looking for, you will find the right person. Have you noticed the common theme here? The hiring process itself requires planning and organization in order to secure the right candidate.

"Test, test, test. This kind of assessment
is your best indication of the candidate's
skills and knowledge."

Seven

Testing

Can the potential candidate pass the qualifying tests or do they freeze up in a way he or she might do on a big sales day?

You need help immediately, *but* don't want to hire the wrong person.

Don't dismiss your gut instinct; it is often the best indicator. Then again the potential employee may surprise you, so don't solely rely on intuition. Testing supports your instinct.

Test, test, test. This kind of assessment is your best indication of the candidate's skills and knowledge. Can the potential candidate pass the tests or do they freeze up in a way he or she might do on a big sales day?

The Hiring Potential Analysis (HPA) is an inclusive test based on tools that have been used for several decades in companies worldwide to determine the workplace personality profile and hiring potential of candidates.

This test is by far the most successful and accurate one test of its nature I have found and there are a lot of them out there. It provides accurate results with which the candidate will agree. You can actually use the results not only in the selection of a new hiree but also for future employee advancement. It is quite remarkable in determining one with a lazy streak, someone who cannot follow instructions well, or one who harbors an extreme resentment to authority.

Another useful tool is an aptitude test, standardized and designed to predict an individual's ability to learn certain skills and be evaluated on the spot. An aptitude test reveals someone's true ability. If a candidate has a high aptitude, he or she can fly through tedious projects that may take much longer for another employee with a low aptitude. This tool is extremely valuable.

An IQ (intelligence quotient) test will reveal an applicant's intelligence level in order to determine who would make better executives. Because a candidate was an executive at his or her last company doesn't always mean that potential hiree was highly effective. A high IQ can determine whether or not an interviewee will succeed.

Testing is an important tool for hiring the right employee. It will assist in predicting the kind of worker this potential candidate will be in six months.

Don't skip this step. You'll miss much valuable information coming straight from the potential candidate. Testing truly gives you an edge.

That being said, all of these steps are important and should be followed sequentially. I know I have said in this book that each step is *vital* and they are, but not exclusively. Narrowing down the initial résumés, comparing résumés to phone interviews, noting first impressions, observing if they hold up in a second interview, detailed reference checks, and don't forget your gut instinct. Be as thorough and demanding in the hiring process as you are in the rest of your business. Stack the deck in your favor and give your business the best possible chance to succeed.

I've compiled as many tests, interview forms, reference questions and procedural checklists as possible into a system you can implement in your workplace. For more, check out the materials section at www.hiringacademy.com.

"It is perfectly appropriate to call a candidate
back as many times as needed."

Eight

Supervisor Callbacks

It's not only a second opinion, but often uncovers a weakness or strength that may have been previously missed.

For business owners and HR managers, probably the single most important component in hiring the right people is what I'm about to tell you. This is *the key* to hiring the right people:

> Be certain that the individual doing the interviews and hiring is an upbeat, productive, and professional person. I have found clearly and undeniably that like people, hire like people. Therefore, if you have a boring, introverted person in human resources doing the hiring, then that individual will hire other boring, introverted employees. This has proven to be an absolute truth.

When a candidate has done well the first time around, send him or her home. After the initial interview, however, invite that potential candidate to return the next day or so to meet with another executive in the organization.

Preferably you should arrange a time for the candidate to meet with a direct area supervisor with whom he or she will potentially work. It's not only a second opinion, but often uncovers a weakness or strength that may have been previously missed.

Observe the candidate when he or she returns on site. Is the prospective hiree again appropriately dressed? Does the supervisor like the candidate? The supervisor is going to work with that potential employee on a daily basis. Is he or she interested in doing so? Is there some weakness about the candidate that the supervisor would like to avoid in new hirees or does some particular strength speak to the candidate's success in the company? Use the supervisor's impressions to narrow down the candidate pool so that filling the position guarantees the business will prosper with a new person on board.

It is perfectly legitimate to call the candidate back as many times as needed. Two or three is always appropriate. As mentioned before, you wouldn't marry someone after a first date. You shouldn't have to trust the future of some important aspect of the company to a stranger. If you're a business owner or senior executive, feel free to meet the candidate personally. This applies to situations in which HR has been handling the previous steps. You should know that your intuition or perceptions are often much clearer than those of employees down the line. The most interesting things can occur when executives examine some aspect that perhaps two or three others have already analyzed.

Here's a wild, but true story as an example. Standing in front of me is a great candidate for an executive position in the company. Good enough that she has passed all of the steps in the hiring process, making it all the way to the president for a final interview. She has an impressive résumé, tested well, interviewed with HR and the area's supervisor, reported great references, fit in with the office culture and seems to be a decent hire for the job. However, you knew there was a "but," right?

She's not a United States Citizen. Therefore, in order to hire her, I have to sponsor her. Sponsoring means I need to sign documents that guarantee her employment for a certain length of time (such as a year) and jump through other hoops for compliance. She, unfortunately, omitted this information from the application. Even with this provision, she seems really qualified and I'm inclined to hire her. Once I read the details of her citizenship issue, I've decided the requirements are fine and our company attorney will easily handle the rest. *But.*

Remember, everything is revealed in the interviewing process. Keep the candidate coming back and either your comfort level will seal the deal *or* the candidate will unconsciously err like this candidate did.

I have her take a seat and cover the pleasantries. She tells me a bit about herself plus her experience and I'm thinking this applicant is a home run. Finally the company has found a competent executive to fill a much-needed opening. *But.*

She then drops a line about how she understands that she's asking us to go out on a limb, so much so, that she has a girlfriend from Canada who had to *sleep with* the owner of the company to assure her job procurement. "However, she was hired", she laughs and looks me dead in the eye as if to say, "Maybe I too, can get the job?" She was *one sentence* away from being hired. It took only one inappropriate sentence to dig a six-foot-deep ditch. The interview ended politely and I asked for the next candidate.

No matter how great your first impression, don't take for granted the invaluable supervisor callback. You have nothing to lose by being thorough and bringing back a potential prospect for a second or third interview.

A Comment on Discrimination

Discrimination is based primarily on opinion but the law usually favors the employee, not the employer, so watch your back. The law is the final word. Familiarize yourself with the basic guidelines to limit legal liability. It may be unbelievable when you read it and you might want to toss some of those ideas in the trash, but refrain. The company can be placed in jeopardy.

Most states have their own laws in addition to the federal codes. Do not discriminate due to age (too young *or* too old), sex, race, and so on.

According to research, approximately seventy percent of unemployment claims, wrongful termination, and discrimination suits are *not* won by the employer.

Never cut corners. Have the company policy manual reviewed by an attorney with employment-law background and make any changes he or she suggests. Document all of your actions, so no gray areas or unclear questions arise about your procedures as they apply to one versus another. Act fairly and equitably with all employees.

Section IV

SELECTING and HIRING

"What was the candidate's greatest accomplishment while working for the previous company?"

Nine

Reference Checks

**Checking references and background checks
are steps often taken for granted, and unfortunately,
for one reason or another, skipped completely.**

I can't stress the importance of checking references enough. By example, when I was an agent in the entertainment industry, we once took on a client for representation just based on "knowing" who he was because he had been in a blockbuster film. Blockbuster mistake. When casting directors were called to get him auditions, to much surprise, they had an adverse response. One finally alluded to his volatility and referred us back to his former agent. One phone call to that agent revealed a story of having security remove this guy from the building after he went on a ranting tirade. We could have avoided this embarrassment, had we just checked-up on him first.

Check the references personally. This part of the process is definitely one step that shouldn't be delegated. Speaking to the candidate's former supervisor personally is a great way to gain insight into the potential candidate and his or her past experience.

Remember when you asked the candidate what he or she thought a former supervisor would say about him or her? Now is the time to bring that question up with the former supervisor. This can prove to be a great starting point if the former employer will talk openly and honestly.

It is not illegal, pursuant to the research I have to hand, for a former supervisor to give a bad reference as long as that person's words are factually accurate. In the past, some companies, in an effort to avoid the headache of nuisance lawsuits, have implemented policies that they will only confirm dates of employment and titles, rather than commenting on performance. Therefore, if you talk to a former employer willing to talk candidly, take every advantage of the opportunity.

The importance of someone else's "recommendation" that you hire a stranger can be instrumental to your future success and it depends on how carefully you question that former employer.

Do not rely solely on written references presented by the candidate. It has been proven ineffective and wasteful to send letters or email messages to former employers as they are likely not to be as candid in writing as they would be verbally, if they respond at all. If companies do respond, they are not likely to do so in a timely manner, which increases the likelihood of you failing to hire a potentially valuable employee.

Don't limit your search for reference information to former employers. Personal references can also be valuable as you might hear a little more about the candidate's genuine personality. Beware, however, of personal references swaying your opinion too heavily. Joe or Jane may be "cool to hang out with" but end up being a non-productive employee and a clock- puncher. Positive praise from a friend is nice but the information you desire from a reference is lauding the achievements of the candidate. From a "personal reference," you are more likely to hear that the potential employee is a good friend and reliable person. This information may not be helpful to the final decision.

Communicate with references via the telephone. Calling provides the chance to ask spontaneous questions based upon your interview with the candidate. Often you can detect enthusiasm, or lack thereof, if you pay attention to the reference's tone of voice.

Sample Reference-Check Questions

You do *not* need to use all of the following questions. Pick a few you feel comfortable asking as your own and that will suffice. (I've highlighted in **bold** my personal favorites.) Take notes while on the phone with the former employer so you can add this information to the prospects folder.

> When did (candidate) work for your company? Could you confirm starting and ending employment dates?

What was his or her starting and ending salaries? (They may or may not be willing to share this information.)

What was (candidate's) position?

Can you describe his or her duties or responsibilities?

Why did (candidate) leave the company?

Did (candidate) miss a great deal of work? Was he or she frequently late?

Were you aware of any issues that impacted his or her job performance?

Did he or she get along well with management and co-workers? Was (candidate) able to work as a team member?

Did (candidate) have other employees under his or her supervision? How effective was (candidate) at managing?

If I spoke to those employees, how do you think they would describe (candidate's) management style?

Was (candidate) promoted while with your company?

How did (candidate) handle conflict, if it arose? How about pressure? Stress?

Did you evaluate (candidate's) performance? Can you speak to his or her strengths and weaknesses?

What was (candidate's) biggest accomplishment while working for your company?

When I asked the candidate what you would probably say about him or her, the candidate said you would most likely say [insert the candidate's words]. Is this accurate?

Would you rehire (candidate) if the opportunity arose?

If I describe the position for which we are hiring, could you describe how good a fit you think (candidate) would be for the position?

Is there anything about which I haven't asked that you feel I should know?

Always thank that person for sharing his or her time, attention, and honesty.

Background Checks

After arriving at this point in the process, congratulations are almost in order. You are nearing the finish line. However, to validate your winning perception, it is wise to do one last bit of due diligence. This diligence could include a background check, credit check or even drug testing. Every state has different regulations and I am not in the legal profession, so I recommend checking your state and federal regulations to determine your organization's legal obligations and boundaries.

Many companies choose to do background checks and credit checks on their prospective candidates. Background checks can ensure claims on résumés are authentic and accurate. If the candidate will be driving a company car while employed in the position, check the potential candidate's driving record and often a drug test prior to hire. Again check your state law but it isn't unreasonable to check for a criminal history on a future candidate.

Today companies also do credit checks to avoid hiring candidates with a history of negligent financial behavior. An employer must obtain the prospective employee's written consent before requesting a credit report. This consent is especially important if you are hiring the candidate and he or she will have access to finances or sensitive financial information.

Be reasonable about the person and the information you're checking. If you find yourself going into an extensive detailed check on every clerk or counter person, you may be doing more work than is necessary. Do your depth of checking according to the requirements of that particular position.

Checking references and background checks are steps often taken for granted, and unfortunately, for one reason or another, skipped completely. *Refrain from doing that.* These checks are similar to the "truth" in a fortune cookie, *if* they were actually real. You don't want to miss the opportunity to read the fortune that could be told on your new hiree.

"You should have found at least one shining
candidate among the pool of prospects."

Ten

The Hire

For one moment, regroup and review
all of the information one last time.

The time has come to assemble *all* the information you have
collected and review it closely. You have a résumé, interview
notes, testing results, reference checks, and you're ready to pull
the trigger on a specific candidate. Stop! For one moment,
regroup and review all of the information one last time.

Pause a moment. Call the supervisor and have a brief meeting to
ensure some aspect wasn't overlooked. Meet especially if
someone on the hiring committee feels you might be settling for a
less-than-perfect fit.

This meeting is "gut-check" time when you accept responsibility
for the decision about to be made. After re-reviewing all the facts

you have compiled on a candidate, if you have too much reservation or hesitation, that's a revealing sign. Go back to the drawing board, or at least back to the last candidate you did feel confident about.

However, if you look at all the information you have acquired from your final-choice candidate and think, "This person was great, a real breath of fresh air who would do well here," then the task is finished. This step is a short but definitely invaluable one. Take that one last look before you leap into a decision you may later regret.

Eventually, you will have conducted enough interviews to have surveyed the field and become familiar with the level of candidates. You will have found at least one prominent candidate among the pool of prospects.

If you have trouble narrowing down the last couple of choices. I suggest making a list of the most important attributes that set a candidate apart from another. Then mull over the last few prospective employees, looking for some trait or characteristic that's better about one yet weaker than the other in a different category.

This is the time where intuition, gut instinct, and plain personal favorites come into play. But don't tell your HR attorney I said so.

Hiring a High-Level Executive

If you are hiring a high-level executive, such as a vice president or director, business owners should always follow the interviews with an arranged dinner. Invite the candidate to dinner before officially closing the deal. Invite the spouse or significant other as well. This invitation can start everything on the right foot and will also provide that last bit of insight into this new person who will be such an important part of the business. This opportunity allows you to discover any positive or negative social traits; such as if the candidate drinks heavily, uses profanity, is crass, inappropriate or obnoxious. There's a time and place for everything but not in the eventual business meeting when they are representing your company on your dime. Trust me, a candidate will open up in ways you never expected at a dinner and you will either like or dislike your observations.

Contracts and Negotiations

Last of all, document everything. The old adage "Get everything in writing" thoroughly applies. Otherwise, it might appear never to have existed.

For hourly employees this documentation may constitute a simple pay request form sent to the accounting department and the new hiree is given a photocopy stating the hourly rate and the expected start date, all co-signed with full agreement.

For salaried executives, a "letter of hire" should be written clearly defining the terms of employment and compensation. For example, define the phrase "100K a year." Is it net or gross? Is the dollar amount per month, per week, per quarter? Do minimum days or hours need to be maintained for the new employee to qualify for salary, insurance, or paid vacation? Are there certain production demands this new hiree will be expected to meet? All of this information must be detailed in the letter of hire so no unanswered questions remain once you move forward with a new member of the team.

Contracts and agreements in the beginning of a relationship can often be uncomfortable but are really necessary to avoid future disputes. This step is an important one and is a great safeguard for your organization when done thoroughly and correctly. If this step is not completed, you're leaving the company open for an unnecessary potential disaster, especially with a salaried individual. Pay structure should be clarified and detailed with each and every benefit and bonus.

Often misunderstandings occur between net and gross, when pay periods begin and end, or the accrual of vacation days, benefits, and so on. These company policies need to be concise and explained verbally in addition to being written, signed and dated, fully understood, and accepted.

An employee manual will contain a staple of information, including all the particulars of the company, that is, the dates beginning and ending pay periods, vacation days, benefits, holidays, and so on; and after reading his or her copy, each new hiree should sign an acceptance of understanding and agreement to the basic company policies.

Then you'll need to know the HR laws of firing, termination at-will, and termination for-cause, so you are comfortably in control and have an easy solution if the candidate doesn't work out.

If you've read this book and followed my advice, I hope you'll have only hired winners.

The Hiring Phase

This part is easy. Call the candidate and say "Congratulations!" Remember that although this hiree is just another addition to the workplace with which you are so familiar, it is new and exciting to the potential employee. A new workplace is a new home and family for so many reasons.

Take the time and forethought to let the candidate express personal gratitude and appreciation for landing a new job. Make certain that this potential hiree is ready to commit and not considering other offers or sounding as if he or she is "settling" for your company.

Gently remind the candidate about the learning curve and ensure he or she is ready to dedicate the time, attention, and effort to excel in his or her particular area. You don't encourage "clock-punchers" on the team. You are focused on customer satisfaction and a high level of service both internally (in the workplace) and externally (to the public).

Set a start-date and time for the new hiree to arrive for his or her first day of work. Let that person know with whom they will be meeting. Make sure all of the paperwork is completed, that all of the *i's* are dotted and *t's* are crossed.

It is advisable to prepare beforehand an exact location or space that is definitively the new hire's workspace. This area should have sufficient supplies and the tools necessary for the hiree to begin doing his or her job immediately.

The area supervisor must then take the new employee under their wing to the degree necessary to ensure sufficient training. Most often overlooked are the idiosyncrasies of the job not written in any manual. "Oh, we always do this and that; didn't anybody tell you?" This is precisely where most new employees fall short of expectations.

Personnel in HR should monitor the new hire's progress and contributions by ensuring that thirty, sixty and ninety day reviews are completed, with the input of the area supervisor. In most states, employment is at-will, so if you didn't get the caliber employee expected and they are not correcting, despite attempts to help, then let them go. We all make mistakes.

> **At-will employment** is the guideline under American law which allows for an employment relationship to be broken by either the employer or the employee with no liability, provided there was no contract for a definite term of the employment and that the employer does not belong to a union.

If all is well and the hiree continues to be effective and productive, then moving forward with annual reviews will suffice and you can enjoy a long, prosperous working relationship with this brilliant new hire. Pat yourself on the back for a job well done.

Section V – Bonus!

THE OTHER SIDE
OF THE DESK

Excerpted from my book
Get Hired! Interviewing Truths Revealed

"The job seeking process begins with
these ten points of direction..."

Eleven

Ten Naked Truths
for Job Seekers

**A smart professional wants to know
the "opponent's" thoughts.
Therefore, this view from the other side of the desk
might be helpful and useful.**

This chapter is a behind the curtain look from the other side of the desk. It is an educational sampling of the knowledge and advice shared with job seeking candidates I coach. This information supplements that which you've already discovered from an employer's point of view.

A smart professional wants to know the "opponent's" thoughts. Therefore, this view from the other side of the desk might be helpful and useful in evaluating prospective candidates.

If a candidate has ever consulted with me, been coached, or taught to interview from anyone in the staffing industry, then he or she knows a few tricks. The job seeking process begins with these ten points of direction from *Get Hired! Interviewing Truths Revealed.*

Truth One

Your Decision Comes First

The first "Truth" is *you* must decide before accepting the interview that *you* want the job and *you* are going to be hired.

More specifically, decide that this is the place where your career will begin, or continue. A career, not a job, should be in your interest and is definitely in an employer's best interest.

It is easily understandable that if you don't have self-confidence as the best candidate for the position, you won't convince an employer to hire you.

Complete your homework on the position and company to gain some knowledge, which will increase your confidence. Today everything you want to know about a position can be found on the Internet. You can find either specifics for that exact position being offered at that particular company or general information about that area of employment.

Before you interview, make up your mind about being hired for the job. Compile a list of the reasons an employer wants to hire a prospective candidate and the reasons you fit those requirements.

The self-respecting decision is that you are the best candidate and you know the reasons why.

If you hesitate for a moment about the reasons a company should want to hire you then consider the following thoughts. You're an honest person who wants to find a satisfying job and will achieve that goal. By reading this book and making an effort, you deserve a shot at bettering yourself, improving your own conditions in life, and taking that level of care to the position you'll soon hold in a company.

Employers value greatly the addition of an individual who cares and wants to make a difference for self and others. Help is the valuable exchange you offer to an area when it needs support. Knowing that, you should be able to make the decision that you are the solution to fulfill the company's needs and land the job. *Make* that decision.

I have conducted countless interviews personally with doubtful individuals not sure if they wanted the job, or any job for that matter. The applicant seemed either non-committal to personal goals or uncertain about the skills and qualities he or she had to offer. No employer wants indecision, especially during the interviewing process. Therefore, maintain a positive attitude.

Truth Two

A Good Résumé Gets You in the Door

"Dear Gentlemen" is a huge cover-letter mistake. No one likes to receive form letters, least of all employers. If you didn't take the time to research the company, the job offering, and the responsible individual handling the hiring, why should that individual waste their time reading your résumé, contacting you, and arranging an interview?

A professional candidate knows the executives who should receive his or her résumé with a cover letter, and addresses them personally. Don't send a cover letter addressed to the wrong company for the wrong position. Yes, I've seen this mistake many times in the past. It really illustrates no genuine interest in the company.

A typical, acceptable résumé is one page, sometimes two if covering more than a decade of professional experience in a field. One page is preferred. Your résumé should be complete, but not provide a historical background dating back to summer lawn-mowing or babysitting as a teenager.

When listing positions, include a brief description of the responsibilities and any notable accomplishments during your tenure. In certain instances list positions held at a company rather than merely providing the company name. If you worked at a company for ten years and climbed the corporate ladder, that should be reflected. Self-employment should be delineated as such, including a description of your product or services and in this particular circumstance have pleased customer testimonials available.

If your name could be construed as male or female, ensure correct interpretation by placing *Mr., Mrs.* or *Ms.* before the name.

Employers tell me they dislike parchment paper and pretentious brochure-like résumé presentations. These types of submissions are construed as phony and are tossed immediately. Use plain white or ivory stock in a quality appropriate for your job objective. Never use colored paper, unless you're an artist, because if it is photocopied the results will be murky.

No spelling errors or typos, please. Proofread your résumé or better yet, have someone else lend a second pair of eyes.

Your résumé represents you on paper. Put appropriate care into a professional presentation.

Truth Three

Like a Boy Scout, Be Prepared

A great deal can be said for the oft-repeated motto of the Boy Scouts of America, Be Prepared. Every area of life benefits from meticulous preparation; the quest for landing a good job included.

The statement be prepared is broad and should be used as such in your preparation. Think about *all* of the different areas in which you need to be knowledgeable while job-hunting, not only for the interview but also during the entire process.

An advance in technology, the Internet, has affected this preparation greatly. When I hear about a new prospect, I Google the name to learn about the potential candidate, and then I check if that person has a Facebook, Twitter, or LinkedIn page. Other little precursory actions can be taken by them to discover the candidate they're really hiring. Don't be tripped-up by an interviewer doing a search regarding you, and lose a valuable opportunity.

Your online presence should be clean and positive. Because you enjoyed the A-Team movie, doesn't mean you need "I pity the fool" as your status update while you're out job-hunting. Be aware, extremely aware, that someone *will* research you and may or may not think your presentation is unprofessional.

Doing your own Internet research on the company will prepare you for the questions about how you'd fit in with the prospective employer. Have specific examples of the way your experience has led you to being the perfect candidate for this opening.

Truth Four

Prep Your References, Duh!

Possibly the worst thing to happen before you attend an interview, or even worse after you've interviewed and the company is interested, is having unprepared references.

Let references know they are on your list and may receive a telephone call. Tell them the type of job you are soliciting and any details you'd like stressed from their viewpoint.

Most people are good about this and generously add kudos for you anyway. Always be prepared, in case your cousin or former boss is "in a mood" when the call comes in and erroneously says something to the effect of, "Didn't he already get a job?"

Better yet, don't use your cousin. Relatives are useless references. Even if you worked at your father's business for the last fourteen years, use the office manager or sales director instead of your father. Make an effort to show the interviewer that you actually had to work to advance, not just show up at the office. The same thing happens if you put "friend" under the relationship of your references, or "was my supervisor, but now still friends." That qualification doesn't give the impression you worked diligently and were likeable, it invokes doubt as to whether or not you were there to complete a job or make friends.

Just list a good credible reference from your previous employment. An HR representative would be lower on the scale, but not a bad choice. The president or a vice president is suitable as is your direct supervisor, who hopefully would rave about your punctuality, eagerness to assume responsibilities, and ability to think outside the box.

Along the line of preparation, don't merely tell the reference once and forget about it. You could lose your dream job because three months later that person says to a reference-checker, "Are you sure they worked here?"

When you're looking for promising, new opportunities, make a refresher call to your references to brief them that they may receive a telephone call and you appreciate their help on your behalf.

It is advisable to have a reference page available upon request, but not submitted to HR until requested. It's customary to be asked for three; I'd suggest having four references prepared in case one can't be reached.

Remember, no Uncle Frank. Use the supervisor of your department at the previous job and the HR Manager, too. Add a professor from a continuing-education class or an attorney with whom you did a summer internship. Those types of references give confidence in reassuring your prospective employer that he or she made the right choice.

Truth Five

Dress for Success

Presentation is always of the utmost importance. Numerous research studies state that a prospective candidate has about sixty-to-ninety seconds to make an impression or be deselected. A sharp appearance, warm smile, and a firm handshake are more likely than any other factors in the interviewing process to gain points with the company interviewer.

The handshake can't be wimpy and project a lack of self-confidence or be sweaty and nervous. It has to be firm and accompanied by a genuine smile. You are projecting an image of confidence and competence with your appearance and mannerisms.

It never ceases to amaze me when a candidate comes to an interview at a professional corporation wearing jeans, a loose-hanging shirt, and sneakers. You wouldn't wear a suit to a mechanics interview but the basic instruction mandates wearing a better outfit than your expected work clothes.

This kind of dress grants respect for the professionals who are considering hiring you and it gives them the opportunity to tell you "there's no need to dress in a suit daily" or words to that effect, rather than not being hired because you dressed inappropriately for the interview.

If it's an office, wear a suit, men and women. Women should not wear revealing dresses, short skirts, or tight jeans. These kinds of dress demean you from the outset and can cause a predetermination of your character that might not portray you accurately. If a male executive conducts the interview he may have a momentary interest in the "eye-candy" but as a professional he'll pass on you for the position. If the interviewer is female, she'll likely be uncomfortable with the interview and refuse to consider a woman who appears to be "sexing it up."

This idea equally applies to men who think they're "God's gift to women." Leave the nightclub act at the door. Don't dress in a tight tee shirt or spike your hair like the latest movie star. Don't wear too much cologne, and *do not* flirt with the interviewer.

Poor personal hygiene is a deal-breaker; so arrive neat and clean, with your hair combed, nails trimmed, wearing deodorant, having fresh breath, and not smelling like cigarette smoke. I'd advise not wearing heavy colognes, aftershave or perfumed hair products either.

Part of your image includes appropriate timing. If you're late for an interview, you're not likely to be called for a second consultation. If an unfortunate incident does delay you, call to reschedule; it may save the hiring opportunity. Leave for your destination early to provide plenty of time to overcome any unexpected adversity. If you've not been in this area before, try a test-run to see how long it takes to drive to the building, park in the lot, and arrive on time.

In addition, do not arrive too early. Ten minutes ahead of the scheduled appointment is perfect. More than ten minutes shows a disregard for the interviewer's busy schedule.

Truth Six

Tell a Story; Be Remembered

What will be remembered about you, after the interview concludes? Your dog Grumpy. And it may just be him that makes you stand out and lands you the job.

Consider the role of the interviewer for a moment; they've sat through twenty interviews with nameless, faceless, walking résumés and the only thing they remember is the hilarious recollection of Grumpy. If you can recount a light-hearted, fun story about your adorable pet or some silly family member, you'll win the day.

Why does it matter? Because the interviewer likes you and can see working with you, or more important can see others being able to work with you easily. That aspect is the most difficult part of their job. The interviewer has to answer to the employees and directors in the area for which you are being hired. With a warm and humanizing story, you've given the hiring committee something more to say about you besides your excellent qualifications.

The point is not to overdo it, but to make a lasting impression.

Truth Seven

Interview the Interviewer

The interview itself will reveal the amount of homework you did concerning the position and your general understanding of the production area for which you are being hired. Look for openings to demonstrate some of this knowledge and your industrious perspective.

Casually remark to the interviewer that you want to clarify your understanding of the qualifications the company is seeking and then roll out your extensive knowledge. This will demonstrate initiative and confidence regarding your role in the future of the company. This knowledge could be as simple as knowing the latest products. For example, interviewing at an advertising agency, you'd want to know the campaigns on which the company recently worked and the way you relate to at least one of those projects.

Once you've shown a savvy interest and intelligence level regarding the company, ask for details about how they go about their process. "What division acquires the accounts? Which people work with clients?" etc.

Now you're allowing the interviewer to picture you working alongside the team. Don't overdo it, but asking the interviewer a few questions can really earn you a gold star for thoroughness.

Truth Eight

"I'm Nervous" is a No-no

Take a deep breath, relax, and smile. Don't express your nervousness to a prospective employer. "I'm so nervous" ruins it right from the start. Even if you are jittery, it is rarely noticed. Remember the interviewer has never met you before and you are your own worst critic.

Extreme nervousness could instantly disqualify you for the position. Some stress may be involved with the responsibilities of the position or in the work environment, and you don't want the interviewer wondering, "If this candidate can't handle a simple interview, how is he or she going to deal with the everyday pressures of this job?"

It may sound silly or outlandish to say, but use antiperspirant or deodorant before leaving home for the interview.

Refrain from talking too much, another sign of nervousness. Don't babble about your life, or any other subject. Be polite and listen carefully to the interviewer's words. Give direct, complete answers to questions, express your knowledge of the subject matter, and demonstrate a desire to gain additional knowledge and experience.

Talking too much will lose leverage for a position as much as saying too little. You have to think about the purpose of the interview and the information the interviewer needs to make an accurate decision.

Truth Nine

"When Can I Start?" is a Yes-yes

It is customary at the conclusion of almost every interview for the interviewer to ask if you have any other questions. Assuming you really want this job, you do have one question.

This question could be one of the most difficult ones you will ever ask. It's right up there with "Will you marry me?" and other classic lines.

"When can I start?"

A dichotomy exists; you are most likely nervous and excited but you need to communicate with resolute confidence. You want the job and as my mother always told me, "You don't ever get anything you don't ask for." So politely, and with a smile ask, "When can I start?" You'll likely receive the usual non-committal answer, "We'll call you" or some other reply. Ask nonetheless. It reiterates your desire and decision to start with a new team.

Truth Ten

Follow Up or You've Given Up

Thank-you notes are essential, critical, and vital following an interview. Always send one, period.

With the volatile economic atmosphere today, the time of executives and human resource professionals is limited and valuable. Keep that notion in mind. The simple gesture of writing to thank the interviewer for his or her time and consideration will speak volumes for your character and may move you higher on the list of prospects.

You may surprisingly be the only interviewee to perform this simple act of courtesy.

Make sure the card and the note are simple, conservative, and professional. It should be neatly handwritten (not typed) on a simple plain blank greeting card or thank-you cardstock.

If you can also mention a fact about you that arose in the meeting, that fact will remind the interviewer of a face with the name. Take heed not to overdo it, though.

A simple "Thank you for your time and consideration" will go a long way rather than rambling on about all the things you forgot to mention in the interview.

Use caution about not making a comment or reference to the personal matters of the interviewer that may have arisen during your conversation. For example, if he or she had received a distressing phone call from a family member and excused him or herself for a moment, *do not* draw attention back to that incident. Remarking that you "hope everything is better with your nephew" isn't appropriate. This type of communication may come across as too personal, even with the best intentions.

The last step requires you to follow up. Some companies become really busy and a day off or a sick day may be the reason you weren't contacted. Therefore, call to see if the company has already hired someone or if you are still being considered. You may just be surprised to find they were just about to call you and want to know when you can start.

Conclusion

If You Really Want It, You Can Get the Job

The whole area of hiring and being hired can be a difficult and emotional process. Don't become discouraged, you are deserving; so remain positive and you will succeed.

I hope this advice has helped you.

About the Author

David Jensen is an author, speaker and consultant. He thrives on helping business owners envision, evaluate and expand upon their own passion.

His executive experience includes President and Board of Directors positions with International Consulting and Banking firms, Human Resources and Project Management in diverse industries. He serves as Executive Director of the Rock for Human Rights foundation and sits on the Advisory Board of Project HOOD among other charitable activities.

"My purpose is to help business owners find and hire the right people so that they can pull back from their business and yet continue expanding." ~DJ

www.davidleejensen.com

CPSIA information can be obtained at www.ICGtesting.com
Printed in the USA
BVOW081455011112

304408BV00003B/1/P